Writing
with
Rosie

Writing with Rosie

You Can Write
a Story Too

Patricia Reilly Giff

Holiday House 🐾 New York

HOLIDAY HOUSE is registered in the U.S. Patent and Trademark Office.
Printed and bound in May 2018 at Berryville Graphics, Berryville, VA, USA.
www.holidayhouse.com
3 5 7 9 10 8 6 4 2

Library of Congress Cataloging-in-Publication Data

Names: Giff, Patricia Reilly, author.
Title: Writing with Rosie : you can write a story too / Patricia Reilly Giff.
Description: First edition. | New York : Holiday House, [2016]
Identifiers: LCCN 2015041844 | ISBN 9780823436569 (hardcover)
Subjects: LCSH: Fiction—Technique—Juvenile literature. | Giff, Patricia
Reilly—Technique—Juvenile literature.
Classification: LCC PN3355 .G54 2016 | DDC 808.3—dc23 LC record
available at http://lccn.loc.gov/2015041844

ISBN 978-0-8234-3882-2 (paperback)

To Winifred Clark Curry,
with admiration and love.

one

This Book Is for You

I come from a family of storytellers. My grandmother loved to talk about her trip down the Delaware River. Eyes flashing, arms waving, Nana told me about her escape from alligators, barracudas and a parrot that stole her red scarf.

Then she'd wink so I'd know she'd made it all up. "Fiction," she'd say. "Such fun!"

On Sundays, my mother and her sisters, Marjorie and Jeanne, told stories too. Sometimes they'd tell them at the same time, laughing as they interrupted each other.

I'd have to choose which one to listen to . . . and sometimes I'd go back and forth to create a new story from what they'd said.

I loved telling stories too.

Nana listened seriously as I told her about the kidnapper hiding in the garage, the next-door cat who knew sign language and the pony who lived in my closet and chewed on my winter jacket.

I wanted to scribble down those stories. I wanted to be a writer! I collected pens and pointy pencils, fresh lined paper and pink erasers that smelled like rubber.

Can you imagine how I would have loved a laptop? But those days hadn't come yet.

It was hard to know where to start. And when I began to put my thoughts on paper, I was embarrassed to show them to anyone. Suppose someone laughed at the sad parts, or didn't laugh when I was trying to be funny?

Eventually I stopped trying; I didn't begin again until I was grown up.

I'm sorry about that. If I could live my life over, I'd write from the time I could put two words together, even though I had no idea how to spell them.

Writing is a joyous part of my life. I want that joy for you too, because we all have stories to tell.

So this book is for you, to help you on your way, to show you that anyone can write a story.

I've tried to think of exactly how I do it. Each chapter tells you the steps I take. It's not very hard . . . if you keep at it.

I hope you'll try.

Wouldn't you like to see your name in print?

two

First, You Take a Person

Here's what I do. I sink down on the living room rug and close my eyes.

Do you think it's peaceful? I wish!

Next to me, my dog, Rosie, seventy pounds, with flapping ears and wildly wagging tail, shreds the newspaper into bite-sized pieces. She scatters them over my face, my arms and legs. She thinks peaceful is boring.

I could tiptoe into the bedroom and shut the door behind me, but there isn't much room in there. Rosie's pulled all my shoes out of the closet. She's yanked the quilt off the bed and the clock off the table.

I close my eyes tighter. Never mind Rosie, or the newspapers, or the messed up bedroom. I have to think of all the bits and pieces and snippets I've saved in my mind for a story person.

It reminds me of the day I began to write a book called *Lily's Crossing*. I had to pick a person, or two. I wanted readers to see them clearly, to know what they were like.

What about me, the summer I was eleven?

It was wartime, and I liked to spy on possible enemies.

At the beach I wore a sailor hat and sunglasses, so no one would recognize me. I slathered on lipstick, thick and red, samples I'd gotten from a department store. Some of the lipstick landed on my teeth, but I thought I looked terrific.

I didn't want this book to be all about me, though. I had to have a boy in there.

What about the kid who lived down the street when I was growing up? My best friend, with his serious face, his mop of dark hair and knobby knees.

What would I call each of them?

I have scraps of paper with names all over them. Names of people I've met, like Ariana Turnipseed and Charlie Nightingale. Names from mailboxes, like Tracy Matson, or from gravestones, like Gideon Gregory.

My handwriting is pathetic. It's too much trouble to figure it all out. So I think of my great-aunt, Lily. I think of my grandmother, whose last name was Mollahan.

So I choose Lily Mollahan for the almost-me girl who'd tell the story. (I call her the story person, or viewpoint character.)

And the boy? I'll use his real first name, Albert. I'll change his last name though, in case he wouldn't want to be in a book.

One more thing. I always give the viewpoint character something to make her a little different, a little unusual. Sometimes I choose a skill like singing, or drawing, or even a love of night stars. I made Lily a writer.

I begin to write about Albert and me. But as the story goes on, something happens. My characters change and grow.

After a while Lily isn't me; Albert isn't my best friend down the block.

They've become themselves.

That's the way a story starts.

It begins with a person or two . . .

Their names and what they're like . . .

And something that makes them stand out.

That's all I know.

You can begin that way too.

three

Wait a Minute . . .

My dog, Rosie, is trying to climb on my lap. She does that when she wants something: a bowl of vanilla ice cream, or a run outside to chase after her enemies, the gray squirrel and the striped cat, or maybe just to let me know she's around. *What about me?* she wants to say.

Yes, what about Rosie?

She's not a person, although she thinks she is.

But could she be a book person?

Why not?

I can think of a dozen books where the story person, the viewpoint character, is an animal. A dog. A cat. Even a rabbit.

How about Rosie? Rosie with her great dark eyes, her sweeping tail, her love of shoes and bits of paper.

Now you're talking, she wants to say.

four

Can You See How I Did It?

This is the way I showed my persons in
Lily's Crossing.

Here's Lily:

> It was Monday afternoon. Lily put on
> her sunglasses, her Eddie Dillon sailor hat,
> stuck a Gertz lipstick in each pocket of her
> shorts, and her notebook under one arm. It
> was a beautiful day, a perfect day, and she
> had something perfect to do.
> > Spy.

And Albert:

> . . . the skinniest kid she had ever seen
> in her life. His hair was curly and thick,
> but it looked as if he hadn't combed it in

a hundred years. She stared at him, his face down in the shadows. A nice face, she thought, even though he didn't want to be friends.

five

Your Turn

Pick a person, or maybe a dog.

Give him a name.

Tell what he looks like. Can you see his face, or what he's wearing? (Even if it's only fur.)

Maybe you'll see something else about him. Braces? Chewed chewing gum in his pocket?

How does he act? Does he worry all the time? Is he funny? Does he always jump around? Is he always in trouble?

Is there something unusual about him?

Think about him. Dream about him.

Make sure you like him.

That's the first step.

six

Put Him in a Place

It's early morning, the best time for me to write. I put my juice and cereal on a tray and carry it into my office. (It's not a real office; it used to be a bedroom.)

In the beginning I wrote in a closet. It was small and cozy, with a little window for spying. I missed it when we moved away.

But I've written in other places too. The corner of the garage. The laundry room. Perched on a wide windowsill, my computer on my lap.

I know a girl who has a terrific place to write. She slides under her bed, shoves out her shoes, the dust balls and her collection of shells. She loops up her bedspread so she can see, but no one knows she's there.

Find yourself a place too, an everyday place, a spot to leave your notes.

Back to my office. Quiet? Of course not. We can't forget about that dog with the orange-red hair, that Rosie.

She stands with her paws on my windowsill, growling fiercely at the gray squirrel. But once she's let him know she's the boss of our backyard, I have to protect my cereal. Otherwise she'll lap it up in two seconds.

She's one hungry dog. But never mind her kibbles. She'd rather chew on pens, on the edge of the computer or a chunk of the chair I'm sitting on. She definitely likes bread.

While I eat, I think.

Suppose my person is Rosie?

Where would I put her?

Then I have it. I'd drop her into my house on Plymouth Avenue.

There's a messy pond on one side of the house, with ducks and geese. Rosie doesn't go too near though. The snapping turtles guard their territory.

It's a neat feeling when I decide on a place for my story. It's always a real place . . . so the whole thing is laid out for me.

Once I tried to write about an imaginary place for a mystery. In chapter one, the girl's bedroom was green. In chapter two, it was blue. She skateboarded down Murdock Avenue in chapter three.

The same street was Linden Boulevard in chapter four.

I had to keep going back to find what I'd made up.

What I made up was my mind! I decided I'd always write about a place I knew, or at least a place I'd seen.

Whenever I go somewhere, I look around carefully. Indoors, I check out the pictures on the walls and the books in the bookcase. I memorize the color of the lamps, the stains on the rug.

Outside, I look at the signs in the store windows, the cars in the street, the shape of the houses.

To be a writer, you have to look at everyday things in a new way.

Pretend you have a magnifying glass.

Look sharply at your front path. Notice the hill of dirt that belongs to the ants that scurry back and forth. How does that hill look to you? How will it look to your story person?

Sadly, those ants look like a snack to Rosie. There go four or five of them.

Focus on the chairs in your kitchen. Can you see the scratches on the legs? And underneath, are there bits of hair floating around? In my house that means Rosie is shedding again.

I always mean to write down those details or

save them on the computer. I tell kids to do that too. I forget, though. Instead, I write on bits of paper that float from the top of my desk and drift under the couch.

Something else: I love stories with blizzards, and snow piled high outside the door. Sometimes I add in rain that pelts the windowsill, or sun that sends patches of light against the floor. I glance up at the sky. Is it cloudy, or navy blue and filled with stars?

Adding in these details makes the place seem real.

Remember, you're creating a world for your story person. How powerful is that!

seven

Can You See How I Did It?

In Lily's Crossing, Lily is coming to the place she loves best. (I love this place too.)

> But then they turned the corner, heading
> for the Belt Parkway, heading for Cross Bay
> Boulevard, and the bridge, and Lily could
> feel the excitement of it, the ocean waiting,
> the sound of it, the roll of it, and it was hers
> for the whole summer.
>
> > Rockaway.

One last thought. How might I write about Rosie's place? Something like this:

> Rosie wandered into the food room that
> Mimi called the kitchen. It had scribble-
> scrabble walls with pictures of cats on

all of it. Still, it was the best place in the house: a box of bacon treats high up on the counter that made her mouth water, a loaf of bread just in reach and a piece of cheese Mimi had dropped on the floor.

Rosie carried the loaf of bread inside and climbed on the blue couch. It was time for a nice snack while she watched the ducks sailing around the pond and those turtles sneaking along the edge.

eight

Your Turn

Think of places you know.

Find one for your person, or your pet.

Let us see what their house, school or park looks like.

Splash on some color. Paint the walls; wallpaper the kitchen.

Take us outside to see the yard, the gray squirrel in the oak tree, the bike in the garage. Look up at the sky. Are there clouds racing along? Or maybe it's a cold day, one to make your story person shiver.

Don't forget to collect places for other stories.

nine

Give Him a Problem

Suppose you read a story about a character who had lots of friends. School was fun and easy. Nothing ever went wrong.

Lucky boy or girl.

Boring story.

Suppose instead, something is missing in the classroom. Maybe someone's money, or a ring. And this character was in the classroom alone. You can guess where the clues point. Solving the problem will make the reader turn the pages.

That's the way a story works.

Something has to happen to your story person, a problem he'll have to solve. It has to be interesting; it might even be mysterious. It has to seem unsolvable.

Finding the story problem can be the hardest part of the book.

Here's what you might do. Get out a pile of paper, or turn on your computer. Have you ever had a problem? Write it down.

Ask your friends about their problems. That's one thing about problems. Sooner or later everyone has one.

As I began a book called *Eleven*, I made a list of all the things that bothered me. My best friend, Francis McHugh, moved away. I hated science and lunch in the cafeteria. I could not, absolutely could not, connect a bat with a ball.

But these problems weren't right for Sam. I wanted his problem to be enormous.

I kept thinking, but after a while I got sick of trying to find a problem for him. It was just too hard.

Maybe I should take a walk, I told myself. I could stop for a praline ice-cream cone with peanut butter cups. Or I could go to the beach. Once I saw a purple jellyfish floating around in the water. I could take my iPhone, get a picture or two.

Stop.

This is what happens to writers when they get stuck. They think about the things they could be doing instead of sitting on a hard chair at a messy desk.

Does that happen to you?

Take a deep breath. Tell your dog you can't fool around with him.

Close your eyes and think.

What if . . .

Yes. What if Sam goes up to the attic? What if he finds something that might change his life?

What if he saw his picture on the front page of an old newspaper, but he can't read what it says?

And there it was, at last. A serious problem for Sam. Solving it will take up the whole book.

So tell yourself that a problem will always turn up, if you think about it hard enough.

ten

Can You See How I Did It?

Here's Sam in Eleven:

But the box was metal and locked, too old to be interesting. He leaned over anyway, and spotted a newspaper clipping sticking out of the edge. He tugged at it but saw that it would rip before it came loose.

He crouched down: large black letters on top, a picture of a boy underneath. The nubby sweater with the zipper down the front looked familiar.

He caught his breath. He was the boy. . . .

eleven

Your Turn

Give your person a problem.

Not a little one that can be solved in two minutes or even an hour.

A big problem.

Something that interests you and will interest the reader.

If the problem were yours, would it worry you? Would you have to do something about it?

And here's something else. The earlier you slide that problem in, the more intrigued the reader will be, the faster he'll want to turn the pages.

Got the problem?

You're ready to write.

twelve

Make Him Move

Is there anything worse than just sitting around? In a story, not much!

A reader wants to follow the story person (sometimes called the *protagonist*) from place to place.

A reader wants action. And moving is action.

The action I'm involved in right now is searching for Rosie.

That dog is trouble!

We'd finished breakfast, Rosie poking her nose under my shoulder to grab a piece of cinnamon toast. I hardly paid attention. I was thinking about the most important sentence in my new book: the first sentence.

Maybe I'd begin with an action sentence.

Rosie walked by with my beat-up sneaker clutched in her mouth. The one with the hole in the toe. She'd made the hole.

That was her signal. She wanted to go out.

How innocent she looked. How well behaved.

I opened the door. . . .

Before I snapped on her leash, she raced down the steps, through the garden, into the trees . . .

And was gone.

With my laptop under one arm, a bacon treat under the other, and the last piece of toast in my mouth, I sped down the back path and around the side of the pond.

"Rosie, look what I have." I waved the bacon in the air.

Bacon wasn't on her mind. Her enemy, the gray squirrel, was!

Rosie barked, jumped over rocks and bushes and circled the trunk of the oak tree.

She moved so fast, she was almost a blur!

But the squirrel escaped again!

I went back to the bench under the oak tree and opened the laptop. If only I could capture that movement in my book.

I saw a flash of what looked like an orange-ice cone. Rosie!

She grabbed the bacon treat, gave me a quick kiss on my wrist and went off again, growling fiercely.

Back to the writing.

I felt like a juggler. Today I was beginning the

writing part of the book. On the first few pages, I had to show the person. I had to show the place. I had to show the problem.

I had to hook the reader in with action.

Rosie was back, panting under the bench.

"I'm writing this for you," I said.

I began to write.

Rosie raced across the lawn, her feet pounding.

There. Was that so hard? Half the morning was over, but at least I'd begun.

Once I spent the afternoon trying to figure out how to make a person sit down in a moving way. An action way.

Lily Mollahan sank down on a bench.
She slid into her seat.
She slumped on the floor.
She collapsed onto the chair.
She fell onto the soft pillows.

There are a million ways to show action. But you have to find the right way for the person you're writing about.

Lily in *Lily's Crossing* is easy. She's always moving from one place to another: the beach, the movies, the surf.

It was much harder to write about Grace in *The Gift of the Pirate Queen.*

Slowly she turned Willie (the goat) around and led her back to her pen.

She followed Willie inside and set the bowl down next to her. Then she snuggled in the hay to watch as Willie nosed into the cereal.

She could feel a lump in her throat. Everything was going wrong. She shivered and curled up a little closer to Willie.

You can see how slowly Grace moves, how quietly. Even her name sounds quiet and gentle. You know she doesn't race around the way Lily does.

And speaking of racing, what's happening now? Rosie isn't under the bench anymore. She's hopping over the stone wall into my neighbor's garden.

Please, I tell myself. Pay attention to your writing. Make that person move!

thirteen

Can You See How I Did It?

Here's Lily in Lily's Crossing. She's just realized that she should be home! Notice how fast she and Albert move.

> They started to run, crossing the street diagonally, just missing an old Chevy with its headlights blackened, its horn blaring at them. They raced past Mrs. Sherman's. "Same cookies," Albert said, breathless, and then around the corner of the As Good As New Shoppe with the dusty hat and coat, the flute and violin in the windows.
>
> By the time they reached the back road, Lily had a pain in her chest and a stitch in her side.

fourteen

Your Turn

Dive into your story!
    This time begin with a sentence that moves—and moves fast. You want the reader to dive in too.

    After all, your person has a name by now. You know what he looks like, where he lives, what he's thinking. . . .

    And now, what is he doing!

fifteen

Make Him Talk

Often it's hard to capture a person and to find a problem for him.

But the best part for me, the writing that I love, is putting words into the characters' mouths: the dialogue.

In the beginning I had to find out how to do it. So I read.

I went to the library, took fifteen books and dumped them on the table. I should have been quieter about it, I guess. I could see another reader frowning.

I sat there reading a page from one book, a paragraph from another. I noticed you had to put quotation marks around anything someone says, to tell the reader someone is speaking. For example:

"Who's been eating that whole loaf of bread?" Mimi asked.

"Woof," Rosie said.

Another thing: writers begin a new paragraph every time a person finishes what he's saying, as well as every time a new person begins to speak.

Here are Matthew and Cindy from the Polk Street Kids series.

Matthew took a huge bite of pizza. "I love this," he said.

"Close your mouth, Matthew," Cindy said. "You look like a cement mixer."

Matthew closed his mouth. He waited for her to look at him again. Then he opened his mouth wide and shut it.

"Gross," Cindy said. "The grossest thing I ever saw."

I enjoy writing paragraphs like those. They're short and perky. The page looks good without a lot to wade through, and the book gets finished faster.

I also like the way writers use the words *said* and *asked*. Those words slide into the sentence like Jell-O on a spoon. No one even notices them. They quietly let us know who's speaking.

If I used *claimed* or *retorted* or *hissed*, I'd be drawing attention to the word rather than what's happening in the story.

Something else: the dialogue has to sound as if someone is really talking.

Sometimes my words sound awful to me. I tell myself that real people wouldn't talk that way.

When that happens, I tuck my iPhone in my pocket. I close the door carefully behind me so Rosie doesn't escape and go down the front path.

From the window I see Rosie's eyes on me. She looks sad. She wants to go to the park too. She loves to listen to the kids talking as much as I do. I shake my head. "Not this time."

In the park I sit on a bench to listen.

"I did not," the kid in the green shirt says.

"You did so," the girl says. "It's a do-over."

That's the great part of being a writer.

You can be as nosy as you please.

If someone says something about it, just tell him, "This is research; it's part of what a writer does."

Anyway, listen to the way people talk.

They don't talk in long sentences that take forever.

They talk in fragments, such as:

Beast flew down the hall.
"Those are school pants?" a voice said.
He looked up. It was Mrs. Kettle, the

strictest teacher in the school. "Just because it's summertime . . ." She shook her
head.

Beast looked down at his jeans.

There were long strings hanging from
the hole.

"I didn't know . . ." he began. "I forgot
that . . ."

One last thing about dialogue. Everything that's
said has to do with the story. You can't just talk
about what your person ate last night, or where he
went last week.

Stick to talking about what makes the person
seem alive.

sixteen

Can You See How I Did It?

Here's Hollis, a foster child, in a book called *Pictures of Hollis Woods*. She's spent the summer with a family she's begun to love. And now they have a surprise for her:

"How can we let her go?" Izzy was saying.

"We can't," the Old Man said.

My heart began to pound so loud I thought it would come through my chest.

A mother, I thought. M.

"She belongs here," Izzy said. "Steven feels it too."

B, belong. G, girl. S, sister. W for want, W for wish, W for Wouldn't it be loverly? My head was spinning.

"I've been thinking about it," Izzy said.

"The winter house in town is too small.
We'd have to put a room on for her."

I don't need a room. A couch. A sleeping
bag.

Izzy and the Old Man are doing the talking here,
rather than Hollis. But it almost seems as if she's
speaking too. Her thoughts are quick, almost as if
she's saying what she thinks aloud.

seventeen

Your Turn

Pull out a piece of paper, or open your
computer. Make your person talk to:

    his mother

    his friend

    his enemy

    Make them talk to him.

    Let him tell about his worries.

    Read it aloud. Make sure the person sounds like
himself . . . the person you picture in your mind.

    Now put him back into his story.

eighteen

Juggling

My son Bill can actually do that. He takes three balls and sets them in motion, throwing two up, catching the third.

In a way, writers juggle the only three things we have in order to tell a story.

There's moving; let's call it *action*.

There's talking; let's call it *dialogue*.

And there's a third I haven't mentioned yet, but you'll see it in Can You See How I Did It sections. It's called *description*.

So we juggle. We hurl in a little action, toss in a bit of dialogue and throw in a brushstroke of description so it all hangs together.

Let's say you're going to the library. You're dying for a good book. You stand in front of the shelves searching, opening one book after another.

One has a solid block of words going from the

top of the page to the bottom. Ah, the whole thing is description. Where's the dialogue? Where's the action?

You toss it back.

Another has a bunch of short, sharp sentences. That's action. But no one's talking. And who can figure out where the action is taking place? There's no description.

That one goes back on the shelf too.

A page in the third book has all dialogue. Even that gets boring after a few minutes.

So the book you pick is one that blends action, dialogue and description. A little of this, a little of that. And the page looks right. Some fast action sentences, a bit of dialogue and enough description for us to figure out where the person is.

You check out the book. Soon you're on your way home to put your feet up and read.

nineteen

Can You See How I Did It?

Here's Sam with his friend Caroline, sneaking up to the attic. He wants to read that newspaper clipping at last.

Sam took off his sneakers and stood on the navy blue quilt that covered the bed. He reached for the rope to pull down the door with its stairway attached. It was heavy and swung down slowly.

He climbed the steps to the top, then crouched on the edge of the attic floor and reached for Caroline. She didn't take his hand. "I can do it," she said, slipping out of her sneakers too and climbing up. "I'm tough."

Tough, his own word.

In the attic, dim light came from the

windows. The flashlight beamed across the floor, its light splashing a circular pattern on the far wall. There were small creaking sounds, the house settling around them. "Breathing," Caroline said.

"Mice," Sam said, to tease her.

They knelt on the floor, trying one key after another. . . . Sam wiped his face with his sleeve. But Caroline looked cool; she sat back on her heels and waited. He tried not to glance at the edge of the newspaper clipping, not yet.

None of the keys fit.

Can you see what I've done? A little of this, a little of that! Action, dialogue, description.

twenty

Your Turn

Let's see you juggle.

Try action. Make your character move!

How about *dialogue?*

Give us brushstrokes of description.

Doesn't the page look good with all those ins and outs? I call it texture.

twenty-one

Make Him Worry
about the Problem

Worry. That's what happens to me when I get part of the way through the story.

Everything stops.

Does it happen to you?

You're going along as fast as you can, the words almost pouring onto the page.

Then suddenly you can't think of anything to say.

What can you do about it?

First a warning: don't throw your story away.

I take myself and Rosie outside. I stare at the patches of ice on the pond. Rosie stares up at the gray squirrel. I try to think about what's wrong with my book.

At this point, someone might ask, "Did you make an outline of your story?"

"Absolutely not," I'd answer. And you can answer the same thing if you wish.

I know some writers, and some teachers too, who like outlines. They enjoy laying out the story like a map.

You might try an outline. It might be easier that way. But I can't make it work for me.

If I outline, my story is boring. Nothing unexpected happens along the way. A person doesn't pop up and say, "Hey, I'm here too. I'm fun and important, and I want you to do something with me."

But back to the story slowdown. Suddenly my person doesn't dance in front of my computer. He sits at the edge of the page frowning at me, not moving, not talking.

I have to backtrack, right to the beginning. There are things about my person I haven't thought about . . . things about his problem I have to learn.

That might happen to you.

Here's what I check (you might want to do it the same way): Take a good look at your person. Can you see him? Can the reader see him?

If not, go back to the living room floor to make him real. Look at his face to see it clearly: the color of his eyes, the thickness of his hair.

How white are his teeth? How big are his ears?

Does he talk softly or loudly?

Does he laugh a lot?

More importantly, look inside his head. What are his thoughts and feelings?

Right now you might discover something.

The story person might not look like you, but his thoughts and feelings are yours.

Yes, I'm a little like Lily in *Lily's Crossing*.

And what about Emily in the Polk Street School books? Her father is a policeman, just like mine was. She has a little sister who's funny and sings a lot, just like my sister, Annie.

The things that worry Lily and Emily are the things that worry me.

Here you are, down on your blue rug, thinking about yourself as the story person and what you're afraid of.

Take a look at the problem. Does it really worry you, or even scare you?

If your person couldn't solve it, would you feel terrible?

Talk to yourself. No, you're not weird; all writers talk to themselves.

Tell yourself it's usually one or two things that make the story stop: a person who doesn't seem real, or a problem that doesn't make your person worry enough.

Which one is it?

Maybe it's both.

You might have to go back to the beginning and add or change things. You'll have to make him worry!

That's what writers do.

twenty-two

Can You See How I Did It?

Remember Sam in my book *Eleven*? He can't read, and he's angry about it, so angry he's dug a letter into his desk. So he's in trouble, waiting in the principal's office for his grandfather, Mack, to come for him. I felt his anger, his worry over not reading, his sadness.

"They left me," Sam said.

Mack had hesitated. "It's terrible to be alone."

"Something in my chest."

"Yes, I know."

He'd looked up at Mack. "Really?"

"The next time you're angry, wait until you get home. I'll show you how to get rid of that thing in your chest." Again that hesitation. "It's what I always did."

In the workroom, Mack had given him a block of wood with three large nails hammered a third of the way in. "Just hammer," Mack had said. "Hammer hard."

Sam had done it then, and dozens of times later. It always had something to do with not being able to read. He pounded in the nails until the block that was in his chest shrank away.

twenty-three

Your Turn

Is your person worrying about his problem? Worrying enough to make the reader worry too?

If not, go back. Read what you've written.

Do you care enough about what happens to your person?

Is his problem really big enough?

Check it out.

twenty-four

And the Problem Gets Worse and Worse

I've left the bacon treats at the edge of the kitchen counter, and worse, the back door is open.

Rosie is flying across the yard, a pair of bacon strips hanging out of her mouth.

And is it possible? Barking madly, she's trying to climb the oak tree, hot on the trail of the gray squirrel again.

That dog gets worse every day.

I slam out the back door and grab her collar, which comes off in my hand.

But the squirrel's back in her nest, a giant hole in the tree, and Rosie comes in for a nap.

Whew. It's hard to get in writing time with that dog carrying on all the time.

Back to the story. In every chapter the problem has to get harder to solve. I call this part making the problem worse and worse; some writers call it *plotting*.

Whatever you call it, it means putting obstacles in your person's path, almost like a snowball that rolls down the hill, picking up more snow as it goes.

It means keeping the reader wondering and worrying. What's going to happen next?

It means making every page so interesting that the reader can't wait to turn to the next one.

I make a list. I put the problem right there on top.

I squint up at the ceiling. What's the absolute worst thing that could happen? I put that down at the bottom of the list. I picture my story person stamping his foot, yanking at his hair, ready to cry!

And then I write in the rest of the list. What will make me get to that absolute worst thing? (It's almost like an outline, isn't it? But not quite.)

As I work on the list, I'm ready to stamp my own foot and yank at my hair. I'm almost ready to cry.

Because once I've gone on with my story, filling in all these obstacles, I wonder how I'll solve the problem.

And you know what?

At this point, I haven't a clue.

twenty-five

Can You See How I Did It?

Here's the first list I made for Hollis in *Pictures of Hollis Woods*. There were more . . . lots more!

- Holly wants to be part of a family, but she's a foster child and goes from one family to another.

- When she's sent to the Regans' for the summer, she hopes she's finally found a family, but she knows she's caused a terrible accident, so she runs away.

- She's sent to live with Josie Cahill, whom she loves, but Josie is old and forgetful and the social

service worker is going to take
her away again.

How will I ever solve this?!

twenty-six

Your Turn

It's time to make the problem worse and worse.

Begin those lists. Don't worry if they're a mess; you're just getting ideas on how to make the problem worse.

Each time the reader begins a new chapter, the story person should be in more trouble.

Pile his troubles up as high as you can.

twenty-seven

And in the End . . .

You solve the problem.

No, not you.

The story person!

His mother can't do it for him, nor can his father. Even his friends must stand back and watch.

The most any of them can do is help just a little bit.

It's his problem after all.

At this point, I call Rosie. "Come on," I say. "Let's go for another walk."

Outside, she pulls at the leash; I run along behind her. She's looking for Enemy Two: the striped cat that lives around the corner. The striped cat that spits whenever she sees Rosie.

I talk aloud to myself. That's why I take Rosie. The neighbors think I'm talking to her.

"What then?" I say. "What does my story person do?"

In my book *Eleven,* Sam loved woodworking but could hardly read. He had to take the first step in solving his problem.

One day, he went back into school and down the stairs to the resource room. "I have to read," he told Mrs. Waring, the reading teacher. "I don't have to be a great reader, but I have to get by."

So that was the beginning: his determination to read. And we can guess, can't we, that he's going to make it happen.

"My person hasn't changed," you say. "He hasn't grown one bit. He's the same old person I started out with."

Take out your story and read it again.

Do you meant to tell me that with everything he's had to worry about, he hasn't become a little wiser?

I bet he has.

And this will help you end the story.

It always helps me.

Let me tell you about a story I wrote. It was about a boy named Richard, who was angry and sad that he'd been left back.

He'd gotten himself into one mess after another: trouble in school, lying.

But then . . . he learns he's been causing some of his own problems.

He can stop running in the halls.

He can do the best he can.

So now he's solving his problems himself.

It was the same way in another book called *Purple Climbing Days*. Now the same boy is supposed to climb the rope in gym. And when he finally believes in himself, believes that he can do it, he begins to climb—not very high, but it's a beginning.

Maybe your story person won't solve his problem completely, but at least he'll make a beginning. That's enough, if he's changed and grown.

It's all you can expect.

The reader will finish the last page and be satisfied. The story has ended in a way that feels right, feels good.

And that's what makes a reader happy.

twenty-eight

Can You See How I Did It?

Here's Lily again, in *Lily's Crossing*. The war is over, and Albert, the best friend she made last summer, has gone back to Canada. So now:

> Lily thought about her problem list for the first time in a long time. Lies, and Daydreaming, and Friends, need. She didn't lie anymore. Every time she started to lie, she thought of Albert and closed her mouth. She still daydreamed, though. Sister Benedicta had told her that all writers did that, and that as long as you knew the difference between lies and daydreams you were in good shape.

And so Lily's changed and grown. She'll daydream her stories into books!

That wonderful writer Betsy Byars once said, "I'm the boss of my book." That makes me the boss of what happens to Lily, and I wanted to give her the last thing on her list: *Friends, need.*

I brought her best friend, Albert, back to Rockaway. I brought him back to her.

twenty-nine

Your Turn

It's time to make your story person do something.

He has to solve his problem.

Take a walk. Talk to yourself. What could he do? What seems right for him to do?

If you don't want to walk, open the computer. Write down all the things you can think of to solve his problem.

One will click.

Sooner or later.

But you'll solve it. . . . I promise.

thirty

And Now . . .
Begin on Page One

Take a deep breath.

You're finished.

Oh, no you're not. You're coming to the best part.

Have you ever been to the beach and turned over a shell that was smooth and polished as you ran your fingers over it?

That's what's going to happen to your story.

You may have to wait a few days to let things settle in your mind. Sometimes you're so sick of thinking about your story person and his problems, that you can't tell what's good about it, or what doesn't work too well.

So take a little time off. Why not? You deserve it after all this work.

But then, look at it on a Saturday morning when it's sunny and you feel happy. Or pull it out on a snowy afternoon when you can cuddle on the couch.

Begin to read.

Do you love your story person?

Can you see his place clearly, or do you have to add a couple of sentences so the reader can see it too?

How about that problem? Big enough? Are you happy with the way it's solved?

Every sentence in the whole story has to belong. Every bit of dialogue has to be about the story.

And speaking of words, get rid of the old tired ones. *Very* is one. *So* is another. How about *but* and *though?* Make a list of the ones you're sick of . . . and remember not to use them yourself.

Check those sentences too. Do they drag on forever, strung together with *and?* Pretend you have a scissors, and snip them down to the size of a comfortable breath.

It's your last chance to listen to those words. Makes sure they're strong, bold and colorful.

And then, at last, you're really finished.

thirty-one

What's Next?

Do you sit back, feet up, to read a book? Or take yourself down the block for a praline ice-cream cone? Maybe you'll walk the dog.

I do all of that, especially taking Rosie outside. She's just eaten the fringe off the couch pillow.

After you've finished reading that terrific mystery, or eaten a strawberry Pop-Tart, or thrown a Frisbee for your dog to catch . . .

It's time to begin another book.

And while I've been writing this, I've been thinking of another story.

Rosie is a great story person.

It would be fun to write about her huge chocolate eyes, her orange-ice coat, her tail so bushy it almost sweeps the ground.

She's one tough customer, but everyone loves her, especially me.

I don't even mind that she jumps in bed ahead of me and takes up most of the room.

She could be a person.

And she has a place too. From the writing room, to the pond outside, to the couch where she spies out the window.

What about a problem for her?

She doesn't have one.

She has a perfect life.

She swivels her head and stares up at me with those chocolate eyes. I think she's saying, "WRONG!"

So what's your problem, Rosie?

Me?

I'm her problem?

I won't let her chase her enemies, the gray squirrel and the striped cat?

I'm stingy with potato chips?

I won't let her dig in the garden or chase the frogs, either?

There was a time I caught her all the way across the road. I could almost picture her carrying a backpack.

Was she moving out?

That's a good beginning for a story, more than enough to start.

thirty-two

Can You See How
I Might Do It?

Rosie nudged the screen door open. It
squeaked a little. It was a good thing Mimi
was upstairs pushing that thing across the
rug, the one that made all the noise.

Rosie padded across the patio without
looking back. She was never going to see
that house again. She was never going to see
Mimi either.

That woman ate a hundred potato chips,
and gave her only one or two!

That woman said, "No, Rosie," every two
minutes.

Rosie was going to run away. Now.

Everything was going wrong. Everything . . .

thirty-three

Your Turn

You know how to do it.
First you take a person.
Put him in a place.
Give him a problem.
Make him move. (That's the action.)
Make him talk. (That's the dialogue.)
Make him worry about the problem.
Let the problem get worse and worse.
And in the end . . .
You know what to do!
Go for it!

thirty-four

Read!

I'm *cuddled on the couch* under my mother's old quilt. Rosie stretches out next to me. She takes up most of the room, her back paws dangling.

I'm happy this afternoon. My book is finished: I've tucked in all my thoughts about writing. And now I'm reading a great book called *Salt to the Sea* while I munch on a handful of Rice Krispies.

Rosie munches too, eating as fast as she can. She's anxious to scarf up the last few crumbs, so she can shred the cardboard cereal box into a hundred stamp-size pieces.

She's impossible, but you know that.

Turning a page I read these words: *a meringue of snow*. Instantly I picture my mother's lemon meringue pie with its foamy white top that swirls and dips.

What a way the author's used to describe snow! I can almost feel it.

I close the book, give it a pat, and put it back on the shelf. "Later," I promise.

I leave the Krispies and the empty box for Rosie and head for my desk.

I have something important to do . . .

Something I forgot to say in my book.

There's more about learning to write. It's reading! Not one book, but many. Tales that are real or imagined, about faraway places or almost in our own backyard, about people who lived long ago or right now in the twenty-first century.

As writers, every time we read, we almost use a magnifying glass to see how the author told her story.

Here's one character I read about: *The biggie kids stand in the back. And the shortie kids stand in front. I am a shortie kid. Only that is nothing to be ashamed of.*

Can you guess who she is?

Here's another one: *I ran down the hall even though the rule is no running in the hall, and I was there in fifty-one seconds.*

The first person is *Junie B. Jones*, written by Barbara Park. The second is *Clementine*, written by Sara Pennypacker. They're unusual, they sparkle. We'd recognize them anywhere.

We might sit back, nibble on Krispies and think. What did those writers say to make their characters stand out? How can we make our own characters jump off the page?

We look for places in other writers' stories.

Here's one from *Bunnicula* by James Howe: *The rain was pelting at the windows, the wind was howling, and it felt pretty good to be indoors.*

I pull my quilt closer around me.

What about *the crook of the moon, the spangle of stars?* from *Homesick, My Own Story* by Jean Fritz.

Here's one by Tomie DePaola: *The water was so high and murky that I was hardly able to* look *at it.*

Murky.

I love that word. It's deep, dark and muddy. You can see what the writer is describing, like the word meringue, or a shortie kid.

Here are words I've read in *Sarah Plain and Tall* by Patricia MacLachlan that I can almost hear: *a hollow scraping sound, a small thump, shuffling and scratching.*

I collect my own sounds: *screeching,* and *moaning* and, back to that torn cereal box: *crack, snap, r-i-i-p!*

There's more to look for.

It's her description of a character's pain that brings tears to our eyes.

It's the worry her character feels that makes our chests tighten and our throats burn.

In *One for the Murphys* by Lynda Mullaly Hunt, Carly thinks: *her look of pity crawls inside me.*

And this is from *Homesick, My Own Story* by Jean Fritz: *Snarling bulldog face, Heel grinding down on my toes.*

When a writer describes an animal's plight, a dog lost, a deer trapped in deep snow, a bird with a torn wing or a raccoon who's starving, Rosie moves closer to me.

I read, tears dropping on the pages, praying the animals will survive.

These writers capture me. Maybe it's because I love Rosie and can't imagine her starving, or lost, or trapped somewhere waiting for me to rescue her.

But it's more than that. Writers make me see the strength of these animals as they try to save themselves. They paint vivid pictures with their thoughts, their words.

That's what it's all about: choosing a word, a phrase, a sentence that shows a world that comes to life.

As writers we're in love with words: heartbreaking, hilarious, frightening or intriguing words.

What fun it is to see how writers do this, how they make us laugh or cry.

Right now, I step over the empty box that Rosie's torn into bite-size pieces. She's taking a nap after all that hard work.

But not me. I want to pull that book off the shelf again. I want to know more about the place with a meringue of snow.

Tomorrow I'll write, but now I pull the quilt around me; Rosie rests her head on my lap.

I begin to read.

Acknowledgments

An enormous thank-you:

To my son Jim who brings piles of books for me to read and gives me ideas too;

To my son Bill who reads my stories and makes suggestions that make a difference;

To my daughter, Alice, who supports me in all I do;

To my grandchildren, a captive audience for my books;

To our newest family member, our Haylee, who'll be ready to read my books soon (I'm writing for her now);

And always to my husband, Jim. If I wrote the dictionary, he'd say he couldn't put it down!

Words I've Used

----

1. Sepetys, Ruta, SALT TO THE SEA, Philomel, p. 2.

2. Park, Barbara, JUNIE B. JONES HAS A MONSTER UNDER HER BED, Random House, pp. 7–8.

3. Pennypacker, Sara, CLEMENTINE AND THE FAMILY MEETING, Hyperion, p. 15.

4. Howe, James, BUNNICULA, Atheneum, p. 4.

5. Fritz, Jean, HOMESICK, MY OWN STORY, Putnam, p. 55.

6. DePaola, Tomie, 26 FAIRMOUNT AVENUE, Puffin, p. 2.

7. MacLachlan, Patricia, SARAH, PLAIN AND TALL, HarperCollins, pp. 5, 60, 44.

8. Hunt, Lynda Mullaly, ONE FOR THE MURPHYS, Penguin, p. 5.

9. Fritz, p. 12.

Books by Patricia Reilly Giff

Novels

Suspect

The Gift of the Pirate Queen

Trail Screaming Teen

Lily's Crossing

Nory Ryan's Song

All the Way Home

Pictures of Hollis Woods

Maggie's Door

A House of Tailors

Willow Run

Water Street

Eleven

Wild Girl

Storyteller

R My Name Is Rachel

Gingersnap

Winter Sky

Until I Find Julian

Jubilee

Non Fiction

Mother Teresa

Laura Ingalls Wilder

Diana

Don't Tell the Girls

Writing with Rosie

Series

Kids of the Polk Street School
Abby Jones, Junior Detective Mystery
Ronald Morgan
wPolka Dot Private Eye
Casey, Tracy And Company
Friends and Amigos
Lincoln Lions Band
Ballet Slippers
Fiercely and Friends
Hunter Moran
Adventures of Minnie and Max
Zigzag Kids

Picture Books

Next Year I'll Be Special
Today Was a Terrible Day
The Almost Awful Play
I Love Saturday
Soccer Song
Patti Cake and Her New Doll

About the Author

Patricia Reilly Giff grew up in New York City where many of her books are set. She graduated from Marymount College, earned a M. A. in history from St. John's University, and a Professional Diploma in Reading and a Doctorate in Humane Letters from Hofstra University.

Before she was a writer, she was a teacher specializing in reading.

When she began writing at age forty Patricia Reilly Giff was still teaching full time as well as bringing up three children with her husband, Jim. Every day she made herself get up one hour earlier to write in a tiny workspace that Jim had made out of two closets. Her first work, a picture book called *Today Was a Terrible Day* came out in 1980 and was translated and published in several foreign countries. In the mid 1980s she began her Kids of the Polk Street School books, one of the earliest and best-loved chapter books series. She went on to publish a wide range of highly acclaimed fiction, nonfiction, and picture books for children. Her books have received many of the most prestigious awards given to children's books including two Newbery Honor awards: one for *Lily's Crossing*, which was also a *Boston Globe-Horn Book* Honor Book and another for *Pictures of Hollis Woods*.

In 1990 the Giff family opened the Dinosaur's Paw, a children's bookstore named after one of the books in the Kids of the Polk Street School series. Patricia Reilly Giff teaches courses in writing for children in the store in Newtown, Connecticut. She lives in Trumbull, Connecticut with her husband and, of course, Rosie, her golden retriever.